Private Peaceful

Classroom Questions

A SCENE BY SCENE TEACHING GUIDE

Amy Farrell

SCENE BY SCENE

ENNISKERRY, IRELAND

Scene by Scene
11 Millfield, Enniskerry
Wicklow, Ireland.
www.scenebysceneguides.com

Ordering Information:
info@scenebysceneguides.com

Private Peaceful Classroom Questions/Amy Farrell. —1st ed.
ISBN 978-1-910949-16-0

Contents

Pre-reading

1.   Based on the novel's title, what do you think this story is about?

2.   Based on the novel's cover, what do you expect the story to involve?

3.   What do you already know about World War One?

Five Past Ten

1. How does the speaker feel about going to school?

2. What do we learn of the speaker's family in this chapter?

3. Why didn't Thomas take the Robin's eggs?

4. Describe Mr. Munnings.

5. What are Mr. Munnings' commandments?
   What is your reaction to them?

6. How did Thomas' father die?

7. What is Thomas' horrible secret about his father's death?

8. What are your first impressions of Thomas?

9. What kind of place is this story set in?

Twenty to Eleven

1.   What do you learn about Big Joe as this chapter begins?

2.   What punishment did Charlie and Thomas receive from
        their mother for tricking Big Joe into eating rabbit
        droppings? What is your reaction to this?

3.   Are Charlie and Thomas good to Big Joe? Explain your
        viewpoint.

4.   How did the boys insult the Colonel?

5.   Why does Charlie fight with Jimmy Parsons?
        What would you do in his position?

6.   How are the boys punished for fighting?
        What is your reaction to this?

7.   "From that moment on Molly became one of us."
        Why is she accepted so easily by the boys, in your opinion?

8.   What does Thomas think of when he thinks of his mother?

9.   Why wasn't Big Joe allowed to attend school?
        What is your response to this?

10.   How did Thomas' mother change when his father died?

11. Why did the Colonel come to their cottage? What is your reaction to this?

12. Why did Grandma Wolf move in with them?

13. What is life like with Grandma Wolf?

Nearly Quarter Past Eleven

1.   Why does Grandma Wolf like Molly?

2.   What present does Molly give Big Joe for his birthday?

3.   What does Grandma Wolf do when she finds this present? What do you think of this?

4.   What "miracle" happens, that rids the family of Grandma Wolf?

5.   Why did Charlie decide to go poaching?

6.   Why aren't the family evicted?

7.   Why wouldn't Thomas swim with Charlie and Molly at first?

8.   What illness does Molly get?

9.   What is Molly's mother like?

10.   Do the children lead a happy life, in your opinion?

Ten to Midnight

1.   Is Thomas religious, do you think?

2.   What goes wrong when the boys go poaching without Molly?

3.   What punishment does the Colonel decide on?

4.   Is Thomas close to Charlie and Molly, in your opinion?

5.   Why is Thomas jealous of Charlie?

6.   "But nothing stays the same." How have things changed between Thomas and Charlie?

7.   What rumour does Thomas hear about the Colonel and Grandma Wolf?

8.   Why did the pilot land the airplane?

9.   Why is Charlie in trouble with the Colonel? Do you think he was foolish to do this?

Twenty Four Minutes Past Twelve

1. Thomas mentions "No-man's land" at the start of this chapter. What does this expression mean?

2. If the Colonel was going to shoot Bertha anyway, why is he so angry with Charlie?

3. Are you surprised that Charlie lost his job over a useless dog?

4. "What a mother we had!" Why is Mother so supportive of Charlie here, in your opinion?

5. Why does Molly stop visiting the Peacefuls?

6. What reason does Molly give Thomas for her father being so strict with her?

7. How does Thomas first hear about the war?

8. Why is war breaking out, according to Molly? How accurate is her understanding of the situation here?

9. Why is the 'Wolfwoman', "ranting and raving" these days?

10. Where does Thomas go to work when he leaves school?

11. Does he like his job?

12. Are the characters affected much by the war at this stage?

13. Why has Molly's mother visited the Peacefuls?

14. Why is Tommo angry with his brother? Is he entitled to feel like this, in your opinion?

15. Has Charlie mistreated Tommo, knowing how he feels about Molly?

16. Is Charlie right to put his feelings for Molly before his brother?

17. What happens Bertha as the chapter ends?
How do you feel about this?

18. Would you like to live in this time and place?

19. What story lines are you interested in so far?

20. How would you describe the relationship between Charlie and Molly?

Nearly Five To One

1.   Does Tommo sound optimistic or pessimistic at the start of this chapter? Explain your viewpoint.

2.   What happens Big Joe that evening?

3.   What does their mother decide they must do?

4.   "everything was pointing towards the same dreadful conclusion." What do they fear has happened to Big Joe?

5.   Where does Molly think Big Joe has gone?

6.   What is it like in the church belfry?

7.   What does Tommo think at first, when he finds Big Joe?

8.   What is the mood as this chapter ends?

9.   Describe Tommo's community.

Twenty-Eight Minutes Past One

1. In what ways is the French countryside different to Tommo's home?

2. After they find Big Joe, how does the Colonel ruin the good atmosphere on the way home?

3. Why have Molly's parents thrown her out?
   What is your reaction to this?

4. Why does the vicar attach certain conditions to Molly and Charlie's wedding ceremony?
   What is your reaction to this?

5. Why does Tommo isolate himself from Charlie and Molly?

6. Why has the army come to Hatherleigh?
   Is this an effective strategy, in your opinion?

7. "It's every man's duty to fight when his country calls."
   Do you agree with this sentiment?

8. The toothless old lady suggests it's cowardly not to enlist.
   How do you feel about this?

9. "I was determined that I would do it." What different reasons does Tommo have for signing up?

10. How does Charlie feel about the idea of signing up?

11. What rule prevents Tommo from enlisting?

12. What will the Colonel do if Charlie doesn't go to war?
Can you understand or explain why he's doing this?

13. "It's been bothering me a lot just lately."
Why does Charlie feel he should join the army?

14. "I've had two years to think on why I decided...to go with
Charlie." Why did Tommo decide to go to war? Do his
reasons apply to modern-day soldiers, do you think?

15. "It seems like I've been in that tunnel every day since."
How do you feel about Tommo going off to war?

Halfway Point
Stop and Reflect

This is the halfway point in the novel, a good time to stop and reflect on the story.

1. What historical facts, if any, do you know about World War One?

2. What other texts have you come across that deal with World War One as a theme? What view of the war did they give? In what ways were they similar or dissimilar to our text?

3. What are the major themes and issues you see emerging in this text?

Fourteen Minutes Past Two

1. "Three hours and forty-six minutes left".
   What is Tommo counting down to, do you think?

2. "Don't think. Only remember."
   Why is the past so important to Tommo?

3. Does their training sound tough to you?

4. Are the soldiers well prepared for war, in your opinion?

5. Describe the atmosphere when they leave England and arrive in France.

6. Describe Sergeant Horrible Hanley.

7. "Charlie just would not give Hanley the satisfaction of playing his game."
   Describe Charlie's character and personality.

8. What was Tommo's punishment for having a dirty rifle barrel?

9. How does Charlie react to Hanley's treatment of his brother? Did he do the right thing here, or was he foolish?

10. How is Charlie punished? What is your reaction to this?

Twenty-Five Past Three

1.   What are conditions like in 'Wipers'?

2.   "We want nothing more than for it to stop."
        Do you think Tommo was prepared for war?

3.   What picture does the author give of the German soldiers
        in World War One?

4.   Why has Tommo lost his faith in God?
        Are you surprised by this?

5.   Why did Tommo think Charlie was dead?

6.   "That's my ticket home."
        Explain what Charlie's injury will mean for him.

7.   What is Tommo's reaction to this?
        Do you understand why he reacts this way?

8.   Who is their new sergeant and what does this mean for
        the soldiers?

Nearly Four O'Clock

1. Why isn't Tommo "lost without Charlie"?

2. How does the gas affect Tommo when he breathes it in? Have you come across descriptions or scenes like this elsewhere?

3. "He lowers his rifle slowly." Why does this German soldier spare Tommo, in your opinion?

4. Why is Pete annoyed when Tommo reads out his mother's letter?

5. Why does Hanley work the men so hard? Is this a good way to motivate them, in your opinion?

6. "I thought of deserting." What makes Tommo stay put?

7. What happened to Anna? Are you surprised by this?

8. Why is Charlie unwilling to talk about home when he returns to the front? Do you understand where he's coming from?

9. Are you surprised that Charlie had to return to the trenches, despite his injured foot?

10. How does Charlie comfort Tommo when he is terrified during the bombardment?

11. "My hands are shaking so much I can hardly reload my rifle." Why is Tommo so badly affected, in your opinion?

12. "I know I am dying my own death, and I welcome it." Describe Tommo's state of mind as the chapter ends.

Five to Five

1.   Are you shocked by the opening of this chapter?

2.   What seems to be going on? Is this what you thought
   Tommo was counting down to, up to this point?

3.   What had you assumed about what he was waiting for?

4.   Why did Charlie defy the sergeant's orders?
   What would you do in his position?

5.   Was Charlie treated fairly at the court martial?
   Are you surprised by this?

6.   Is the scene between the brothers moving? Explain.

One Minute To Six

1. How does Tommo imagine Charlie dying?
    What does this tell you about how he views his brother?

2. "They tell me that he refused the hood, and that they
    thought he was singing when he died."
    How does this make you feel?

3. What music would best accompany this scene in a film?
    Explain your choice.

Postscript

1.   How does this information affect you?

Reflections

1.   What view of war is presented in this novel? Include examples in your answer.

2.   How does Charlie's death make you feel?

3.   Is this story similar to any other texts that deal with the theme of war that you have come across?

4.   What did you like about this story?

5.   What actors would you choose to play the roles of Tommo, Charlie, Molly and Sergeant Hanley in a film of this story? Write a paragraph to support each of your choices.

6.   World War One broke out over a hundred years ago. Has warfare changed much in that time? Explain your answer.

7.   Is war necessary? Support your views with examples.

SCENE BY SCENE TEACHING GUIDES

Scene by Scene Series

Hamlet Scene by Scene

King Lear Scene by Scene

Macbeth Scene by Scene

Romeo and Juliet Scene by Scene

Shakespeare Scene by Scene Volume 1

A Doll's House Classroom Questions

Animal Farm Classroom Questions

Foster Classroom Questions

Good Night, Mr. Tom Classroom Questions

Martyn Pig Classroom Questions

Of Mice and Men Classroom Questions

Pride and Prejudice Classroom Questions

Private Peaceful Classroom Questions

The Fault in Our Stars Classroom Questions

The Old Man and the Sea Classroom Questions

The Outsiders Classroom Questions

To Kill a Mockingbird Classroom Questions

The Spinning Heart Classroom Questions

Visit www.scenebysceneguides.com to find out more about Scene by Scene Classroom Questions teaching guides and workbooks.

Printed in Great Britain
by Amazon

35210297R00020